For my daughter Rachel,
who hates scary things,
loves wonderful things, and
recognizes that some things are . . . both.

WORLDVIEW GUIDE

DRACULA

Grant Horner

canonpress
Moscow, Idaho

Published by Canon Press
P.O. Box 8729, Moscow, Idaho 83843
800.488.2034 | www.canonpress.com

Grant Horner, *Worldview Guide for Dracula*
Copyright ©2019 by Grant Horner.
Cited page numbers come from the Canon Classics edition of the novel (2016),
www.canonpress.com/books/canon-classics.

Cover design by James Engerbretson
Cover illustration by Forrest Dickison
Interior design by Valerie Anne Bost and James Engerbretson

Printed in the United States of America.

A free end-of-book test and answer key are available for download at
www.canonpress.com/ClassicsQuizzes

Library of Congress Cataloging-in-Publication Data
Horner, Grant, 1964- author.
Dracula worldview guide / Grant Horner.
Moscow, Idaho : Canon Press, [2019]
LCCN 2019011329 | ISBN 1591282667 (paperback : alk. paper)
LCSH: Stoker, Bram, 1847-1912. Dracula.
Classification: LCC PR6037.T617 D7834 2019 | DDC 823/.8--dc23
LC record available at https://lccn.loc.gov/2019011329

19 20 21 22 17 18 9 8 7 6 5 4 3

CONTENTS

INTRODUCTION

"Denn die Todten reiten Schnell."
For the dead travel fast.

Bram Stoker's 1897 Gothic novel, *Dracula*, features many of the most powerful tropes in fictional narrative: suspense, love, seduction, heroism, sacrifice, and the burning desire for some form of immortality.

Deeply contrasting settings—East and West, London and Transylvania, the sophisticated city and the wild mountains, aristocratic mansions and dank vaults, a happy home and a lunatic asylum—present a binary world that finds its ultimate formulation in the eternal conflict between good and evil.

The long train journey of young English solicitor Jonathan Harker as he enters Transylvania clarifies this bifurcation in the opening paragraph: "The impression I had was that we were leaving the West and entering the East."

The undead vampire Dracula's plan is to abandon the East and invade the West, leaving his crumbling mountain castle for the vitality of central London in search of fresh blood and new life.

THE WORLD AROUND

"Ah, it is the fault of our science that it wants to explain all; and if it explain not, then it says there is nothing to explain."

The end of the nineteenth century, often referred to in intellectual history as the *fin de siècle*, was a complex period of competing forces—political, cultural, and technological.[1] Hopes for the new twentieth century were mingled with dread and fear that found embodiment a few years later in the First World War, as Europe essentially destroyed an entire generation of young people. The Victorian era of England (1837—1901) and its famous obsession with public morality also saw the rise of industrialization,

---

1. The French term for "end of the century" came to mean a general malaise, cynicism, and pessimism at the turn of the century in Europe. This was in opposition to a longstanding nineteenth-century view that progress was inevitable and optimism justifiable in the face of the power of ever-increasing scientific rationalism, which was able to explain the world and bring it under control for man's benefit.

a massive population shift from country to city, and the rapid growth of science, rationalism, and optimism—all linked together as the precursor of twentieth-century Modernism. This positivity was often critiqued by more pessimistic observers.

Some who were not so optimistic about Rationalism developed an increasing interest in revived Romanticism and mysticism, elevating subjective experience and somewhat paralleling the dark Gothicism of the late 18th and early 19th centuries. Cheap, terrifying, sensational novels—"penny dreadfuls"—sold briskly. Industrialization had raised the general standard of living greatly, though many were still living in miserable conditions, even in cosmopolitan London. Eastern Europe served as a geopolitical bulwark against various threats, real and imagined, from the non-European East, primarily identified with the declining but still powerful Ottoman Empire. As a result, a strange kind of "invasion literature" began to take shape, featuring frightening encroachment of the civilized West by the strange and barbaric East. Paralleling this was the long, slow battle between science and superstition, which had been simmering since Sir Francis Bacon invented inductive rationalism or "the scientific method" in the seventeenth century at the end of the Renaissance.

This is the world of *Dracula*.

ABOUT THE AUTHOR

Abraham Stoker was born November 8, 1847 near Dublin, Ireland to an Anglican Protestant family. He was bedridden with some kind of unknown illness until he was seven, and he later claimed that this grew his vivid imagination as he had little to do but read and think. He was educated at Trinity College where he earned high honors across the curriculum and as an athlete. He later became for twenty-seven years the manager of the Lyceum Theater in London, a major theatrical venue and locus of high London society. This placed Stoker among the fashionable elite of his city, and he met Oscar Wilde, Sir Arthur Conan Doyle, James McNeill Whistler, and Americans like Teddy Roosevelt and Walt Whitman. He married the famously beautiful Florence Balcombe, who had been courted by Wilde. There is some indication that the marriage was neither happy nor intimate, though the Stokers had one child, Noel, born 1879.

Stoker was interested in science and progress but also had a long fascination with the occult and all things mysterious or supernatural, and wrote stories early in his career reflecting these interests. At least seven years of intense research and writing preceded the completion of his most famous work, *Dracula* (1897); these research and composition notes survive and have been the subject of much scholarly attention as has Stoker's heavily annotated original typescript of the novel, which was purchased by tech billionaire Paul Allen.[2]

Later in his career, his reputation well-established, he wrote *The Lady of the Shroud* (1909) and *The Lair of the White Worm* (1911), both macabre horror novels which did not have anywhere near the impact of *Dracula*. In fact, Stoker's international literary reputation rests almost entirely upon *Dracula*, which places him among the most influential authors of the Victorian Gothic. Stoker died on April 20, 1912 after a stroke. His widow lived until 1937, and was involved in a protracted series of legal fights over a copyright issue: in 1922 German director F.W. Murnau made *Nosferatu*, a silent vampire movie based closely upon Stoker's novel. When Florence Stoker found out, she sued for damages and attempted to gain possession of all the prints and negatives to destroy them. Some copies survived and the film has gone on to become a classic of the genre.

2. Alison Hewitt, "10 Questions: Dracula expert Leslie Klinger," *UCLA Newsroom*, October 28, 2011, http://newsroom.ucla.edu/stories/10-questions-for-dracula-expert -218133 (accessed on June 1, 2017).

WHAT OTHER NOTABLES SAID

Dracula was not, at first, a particularly good seller, even though Gothic tales of suspense, the supernatural, and horror were wildly popular at the time. Literary reviews were mixed, with some praising the book's eerily atmospheric tone and others saying Stoker went too far with the horror, or the subtle sexuality, or both. However, within a few years the book gained a significant following due to its hypnotic power and creeping sense of dread—the hallmarks of High Gothic.

A sampling of contemporary reviews:

Derby Mercury June 23, 1897:
"Mr. Bram Stoker's *Dracula* … will suit readers who delight in literary nightmares."

Athenaeum June 26, 1897:

"Stories and novels appear just now in plenty stamped with a more or less genuine air of belief in the visibility of supernatural agency. The strengthening of a bygone faith in the fantastic and magical view of things in lieu of the purely material is a feature of the hour, a reaction—artificial, perhaps, rather than natural—against late tendencies in thought. Mr. Stoker is a purveyor of so many strange wares that '*Dracula*' reads like a determined effort to go, as it were, "one better" than others in the same field. How far the author is himself a believer in the phenomena described is not for the reviewer to say. He can but attempt to gauge how far the general faith in witches, warlocks and vampires—supposing it to exist in any general and appreciable measure—is likely to be stimulated by this story. The vampire idea is very ancient indeed, and there are in nature, no doubt, mysterious powers to account for the vague belief in such things. Mr. Stoker's way of presenting the matter, and still more the matter itself, are of too direct and uncompromising a kind. They lack the essential note of awful remoteness and at the same time subtle affinity that separates while it links our humanity with the unknown beings and possibilities hovering on the confines of the known world. '*Dracula*' is highly sensational, but it is wanting in the constructive art as well as in the higher literary sense."

British Weekly July 1, 1897:

"One of the most interesting and exciting of recent novels is Mr. Bram Stoker's *Dracula*. It deals with the ancient mediaeval vampire legend, and in no English work of fiction has this legend been so brilliantly treated. The scene is laid partly in Transylvania and partly in England. The first fifty-four pages, which give the journal of Jonathan Harker after leaving Vienna until he makes up his mind to escape from Castle Dracula, are in their weird power altogether unrivalled in recent fiction."

Letter to Bram Stoker from Arthur Conan Doyle August 20, 1897:

"My dear Bram Stoker,

I am sure that you will not think it an impertinence if I write to tell you how very much I have enjoyed reading *Dracula*. I think it is the very best story of diablerie which I have read for many years. It is really wonderful how with so much exciting interest over so long a book there is never an anticlimax. It holds you from the very start and grows more and more engrossing until it is quite painfully vivid. The old Professor is most excellent and so are the two girls. I congratulate you with all my heart for having written so fine a book."

SETTING, CHARACTERS, AND PLOT SUMMARY

Dracula is an epistolary novel; that is, it is not told as a standard third-person narration (e.g., "She went right in there and told him the truth, not realizing what might happen next") or straight first-person narration ("I woke up, and when I realized what I had done I was filled with remorse"). Instead, Stoker presents us with a fictional series of diary entries, letters, ships' logs, newspaper clippings, telegrams, and so forth, as if the reader is just discovering a collection of evidence which tells the story indirectly. Thus the narrative point of view is always shifting and may not always be reliable or complete. This can be disorienting at first but is very effective in building suspense and a sense of terror about the unknown, as the reader makes connections that the characters do not.

Setting

Stoker's novel uses a pair of opposed settings to heighten the tension of the narrative: mysterious Transylvania and rational London. The novel moves back and forth between these locations several times, so the reader experiences in detail:

• The rustic, backwards, superstitious region of Transylvania, particularly the wild Carpathian mountains and Castle Dracula, the creepy, dark, crumbling home of Count Dracula.

• London, the largest city in Europe for most of the nineteenth century. It is wealthy, urbane, sophisticated, and the center of Western civilization, the British Empire, commerce, science, and rationality. Individual locations include several aristocratic homes of the educated elite, a lunatic asylum run by Dr. Seward, and Carfax Abbey, the new home of Dracula. Carfax, an abandoned structure, is much like Dracula's creepy castle in Transylvania.

Character List

Count Dracula is an ancient vampire who lives in his crumbling castle in Transylvania. He is running low on local victims, so he decides to move to London to feed. Though he is a rhetorically charming and brilliant aristocrat, his real nature is shown to be an absolutely evil, selfish predator who keeps his own immortal life at the cost of others. He can turn himself into a variety of animals, can crawl down the side of a building like a lizard, and can control some of his still-living victims through a kind of long-distance hypnosis. As powerful as he is, his power has limits: he is weakened by daylight and so is nocturnal; he cannot cross water by himself and cannot enter a home unless invited. He is presented as an interesting but entirely unsympathetic character.

Professor Abraham Van Helsing is a Dutch scientist, occult expert, and vampire hunter. His student Dr. Seward calls him to treat Lucy Westenra, and Van Helsing recognizes almost immediately that rational, scientific Western medicine will not cure her. He is the central hero, just as Dracula is the villain.

Jonathan Harker is a young, naïve lawyer who travels to Transylvania to complete paperwork for Dracula's acquisition of Carfax Abbey in London. Though he is first presented as a "naïve narrator"—understanding less than the reader does—he soon becomes a heroic figure.

Mina Murray, a schoolteacher, is Harker's fiancée. She is dear friends with Lucy Westenra, who, like Mina, is victimized by the vampire. She is the novel's heroine, assisting the vampire hunters with her research and insights, and she is characterized by virtue, wit, and strong

Christian faith in the triumph of God and goodness over evil. She in many ways represents the perfect Victorian woman: chaste and pure, devoted to her man, filled with faith and charity.

Lucy Westenra is Mina Harker's close friend and Dracula's first major victim in London. Like Mina she exemplifies the purity and virtue of an idealized Victorian woman—but then she comes under the spell of Dracula, who turns her into a vile undead vampire herself. The transformation is one of the more terrifying aspects of the novel.

Dr. John Seward, a former student and protégé of Van Helsing, runs an insane asylum not far from Dracula's new home, Carfax Abbey. He asks Lucy to marry him but his proposal is rejected; nevertheless he cares for her health valiantly after she falls ill due to the repeated vampiric attacks, which slowly drain her blood and threaten to turn her into one of the undead. While all of this is going on, Dr. Seward is studying the behavior and ideas of his asylum patient Renfield, who eats insects and vermin in order to take on their life force. Unbeknownst to Seward and the others, the strange Renfield is under the control of Dracula.

Arthur Holmwood, a young man from an aristocratic family, is engaged to Lucy. He joins the fight against Dracula and heroically gives blood transfusions to Lucy to save her life—even as Dracula drains her blood again every night. Eventually he agrees to destroy her evil vampiric body in order to set her free from the curse of being eternally undead.

Quincey Morris is a heroic, straight-talking cowboy from Texas, and another of Lucy's suitors. Holmwood wins Lucy's hand, but he and Quincey remain friends. The Texan is involved in the valiant fight against Dracula, and eventually sacrifices himself in the grim task.

Mr. Renfield is an apparently harmless but hopelessly mad inmate in Dr. Seward's asylum. He appears as a slight gentleman but is also preternaturally strong. He is obsessed with gaining the vital life force of other creatures by eating them, though his diet consists merely of insects and vermin which he is able to catch in his cell. He would like something larger, he makes clear. Renfield, an earlier victim of Dracula, is under the telepathic power of his master, who uses Renfield to spy on and counter his enemies.

Plot Summary

Jonathan Harker travels through the strange wilds of Transylvania to complete a real estate deal with a local nobleman named Dracula. The locals warn him about a deadly creature that lives by drinking the blood of the living. Harker is disturbed by these superstitions but is not afraid. After a terrifying carriage ride up into the Carpathian mountains, Harker meets the elderly, urbane Count, who is eager to learn all about London in preparation for moving there. Before long Harker realizes he is not a guest in Castle Dracula—he is a prisoner, desperate to escape.

Back in England, Lucy Westenra discusses her many suitors with her friend Mina Murray, fiancée of Harker. Lucy is found sleepwalking one night in a cemetery, apparently being victimized by a mysterious red-eyed creature. Not long before this a derelict ship had washed up nearby—the crew gone and the captain dead. The only cargo was fifty boxes of dirt sent from Transylvania. Lucy becomes ill, and Dr. Seward calls on his mentor Van Helsing to provide a diagnosis. He notices the two puncture wounds in her neck and her lack of vitality and concludes she is the victim of a vampire.

Harker shows up ill in Budapest and Mina goes to him. Lucy begins to recover slightly after Van Helsing fills her room with garlic, which repels vampires, but eventually she begins to succumb. Heroic blood-transfusions help, but only temporarily—Dracula is draining her blood faster than it can be replaced. She is eventually killed. Van Helsing takes Seward, Holmwood, and Quincey to her tomb, and tells them she is an Undead—a vampire. They catch her preparing to feed on a child and decide she must be destroyed. A stake is driven through her heart and she is beheaded.

Jonathan and Mina, newly married, return to England. Mina is especially helpful to van Helsing in assembling all the information about Dracula, and the little band vows to destroy him. They work to destroy his boxes of earth, which are his sanctuary, but Dracula then manages to begin preying on Mina; he is helped in his activities by Renfield, who acts as a spy for Dracula. As Mina begins to turn into a vampire, too, the heroes chase Dracula back to Transylvania where he is finally killed. Quincey dies in the effort, though Mina is rescued and recovers.

WORLDVIEW ANALYSIS

The opening and closing of the nineteenth century saw the production of two of modern literature's greatest mythic works of fear and dread: Mary Shelley's *Frankenstein* (1818) and Bram Stoker's *Dracula* (1897). The former was written by a teenage lady; the latter by a middle-aged man. Mary, writing in Switzerland, was an essentially exiled young woman in a highly unorthodox and scandalous relationship with an older man, while Bram was a successful and married member of the London cultured classes. Stoker in many ways exemplified the circumspect Victorian era, while Shelley was a classic Romantic rebel like her poet husband, Percy. *Frankenstein* tells the story of a creator and his tortured creature, made by science but formed as a monster unfit for society; *Dracula* features a nobleman accursed with an eternal life that must be purchased by drinking the blood of an endless train of innocent victims. Both tales deal with universal themes of life and death, morality and immortality, and good and evil. Both novelists use the device of multiple narrative perspectives to add depth, complexity, and richness to their stories. Each story is deeply unsettling in its own way, and part of what makes them so simultaneously disturbing and fascinating is the way the authors manage to force us to wrestle with important spiritual questions. While Shelley clearly rejected orthodox Christianity, Stoker's position is more ambiguous. Yet both writers deal with some of the very questions that the Bible is concerned with. What is good? What is evil? What is life, and where does it come from? And is life eternal—or somehow limited? The ultimate question being, of course, *what is man*?

What both novels share is an undeniable mythmaking power. Cultural production is filled with various kinds of myths, which are stories we tell ourselves to explain ourselves to ourselves—our origin, purpose, and end. Myths are not necessarily fictional in the loosest sense of the word; they are true in a larger manner, like the parables of Jesus, which speak truth as fictional representations of eternal realities.

Myths that are forgotten have lost their power over us. Even rank pagans can recite many of Jesus' most famous parables, and the fables of Aesop, and the plotline of *Oedipus Rex*.[3] Things that frighten us remain impressed on our later thoughts. Horror and fantasy narratives are

---

3. Please note that I am not equating these stories but, rather, comparing how they work in human culture.

especially powerful forms of mythmaking because they leave such a powerful impression upon our minds. And *Dracula* is undeniably frightening, as students who have taken my course in Gothic Literature will attest. Many are shocked at just how deeply frightening a bunch of black marks on paper can be.

Part of the terror in *Dracula* is the idea of an "invasion" from a foreign force, in this case "the East" as well as "the Undead." The strangeness of Southeastern Europeans, with their superstitions and barbarian ways, struck terror into the hearts of the Londoners, safe in their rational, scientific modernity. The novel is filled with sentiments like this: "And yet, unless my senses deceive me, the old centuries had, and have, powers of their own which mere 'modernity' cannot kill" (ch. 3, p. 47)." Similarly: "We are in Transylvania, and Transylvania is not England. Our ways are not your ways, and there shall be to you many strange things. Nay, from what you have told me of your experiences already, you know something of what strange things there may be" (ch. 2, p. 30). Ironically enough, it was out of a minor squabble in Southeastern Europe that World War Two would erupt half a generation later, killing more people than an army of vampires ever could.

Dracula and *Frankenstein* have both—quite ironically— transcended their nineteenth-century textual lives and entered the realm of the greatest art form of the twentieth century: film, which creates a certain kind of immortality. Charlie Chaplin has been dead for years, but we can still watch the antics of the Little Tramp decades later. He lives. Bela Lugosi and Boris Karloff (and many of the others who played the undead vampire and the re-animated creature) are long gone—but they still walk, threaten, and terrify through their celluloid and electronic eternal life, a kind of analog and digital reincarnation that inhabits our nightmares. *Dracula* and *Frankenstein* have each inspired well over 200 films. And that is what the most powerful kind of cultural myth does: like Shelley's and Stoker's creatures, *it does not die*.

Where does this fascination with the frightening come from? Why in the world would people invest time and money for books, movies, thrill rides, which serve to create an emotional state that we all naturally find unpleasant? Why would anyone enjoy fear as entertainment?[4]

There is little precedent for this sort of cultural production before the end of the eighteenth century. The "pity

---

4. I have treated this issue at length in *Meaning at the Movies* (Wheaton, IL: Crossway, 2010). I argue that man's suppression of the truth about God and his world as seen in Romans 1 takes root in the heart of fallen man. Man knows there is a holy God to whom he is accountable and hates this inbuilt knowledge as it causes him to live in fear under a guilty conscience. Man suppresses the truth of this reality and yet because truth can never be fully suppressed it returns in another form. In the case of what I call "fear for pleasure" man has built an entire industry around providing a fear that is safe and manageable and entertaining as opposed to a fear of God as terrifying judge. We are made to fear God; we do not in fact fear Him; we have replaced deeply fearing a real God with the enjoyment of fearing unreal monsters.

and fear" that Aristotle says Tragedy should invoke[5] was not the same thing as we see in Gothic literature, ghost stories, or movies like *The Exorcist*. The Greeks wrote tragedies and comedies—but not horror plays. Chaucer wrote humorous medieval tales—not frightening ones. Renaissance drama could be suspenseful and gory, but it was not terrifying. Scholars trace the Gothic back to the widespread reporting of the Reign of Terror (1793–4) during the French Revolution in English newspapers each day. At least 16,000 people were executed in a single year—mostly by guillotine. These gory stories from France, combined with the powerful tenets of Romanticism, seemed to produce a strange cultural phenomenon: fascination with fear, dread, horror, and terror. We could experience fear vicariously (from the safety of our reading chairs) as we watched characters in fear.

This prepared the way for a number of novels and tales in the 18th and 19th century including Horace Walpole's *The Castle of Otranto* (1764, widely considered the first Gothic novel), Anne Radcliffe's *The Mysteries of Udolpho* (1794), Sheridan LeFanu's deeply creepy *Carmilla* (1871), Bram Stoker's *Dracula* (1897), Mary Shelley's *Frankenstein* (1818) and Robert Louis Stevenson's *The Strange Case of Dr. Jekyll and Mr. Hyde* (1886) as well as shorter works by the nineteenth century Americans Hawthorne and Poe, to mention just the best known. The popular twentieth century fiction of H.P. Lovecraft, Dean R. Koontz,

5. Aristotle, *Poetics* VI.

Stephen King, and Peter Straub, alongside an endless series of gore-horror films which bear little resemblance to
the literary and philosophical depth of either Stoker or
Shelley, show that the genre has cultural sticking power.

But why?

Edmund Burke's famous 1757 essay *A Philosophical En-
quiry into the Origin of Our Ideas of the Sublime and Beautiful* first described in intellectual terms the experience of
terror and awe in the face of the unknown, the powerful,
and the threatening. His distinction in aesthetics between
the *Beautiful* (that which pleases us by its form) and the
Sublime (that which overwhelms us utterly by its power) provide a central point of entry into any study of the
imaginative use of fear for pleasure. Burke built his argu-
ment on top of the work of the ancient Greek philosopher
Longinus, who wrote *On the Sublime* in the 1st century
AD. According to Longinus, the Sublime "transports us"
out of ourselves. The Grand Canyon fills us with awe of
its beauty as well as terror of its danger. Related to and
arising partly out of German and British Romanticism
and the renewed fascination with the idea of the Sublime,
"The Gothic" encompasses both style and content and
makes a distinction between "Terror" (anxiety and dread)
and "Horror" (fear and shock). Terror, in Burkean terms,
is: "Oh no—what's next??" Horror is: "Oh no—it's here
and I can't bear it!!" Hitchcock's suspense films create terror, while Wes Craven makes *horror* movies. Terror won-
ders what is behind the curtain; horror pulls the curtain

back and shoves you forward into the unnameable. We are simultaneously attracted and repulsed; we cannot look, and we cannot look away.

Dracula is a novel filled with both terror and horror, and so exemplifies the Gothic in its fullest form. Suspense at what may come is followed by revulsion at what has arrived. The destruction of the corporeal form of Lucy's vampiric body is a moment of almost unbearably nauseating violence (ch. 16). Holmwood drives a stake through her heart after she had called him her husband and invited him, in a grotesquely erotic manner, to come to her. She is then decapitated and her mouth stuffed with garlic.

Harker's earlier encounter with the three vampire women in the castle is another such scene.

> There was something about them that made me
> uneasy, some longing and at the same time some
> deadly fear. I felt in my heart a wicked, burning de-
> sire that they would kiss me with those red lips....
> I was afraid to raise my eyelids, but looked out and
> saw perfectly under the lashes. The girl went on her
> knees, and bent over me, simply gloating. There was
> a deliberate voluptuousness that was both thrill-
> ing and repulsive, and as she arched her neck she
> actually licked her lips like an animal, till I could
> see in the moonlight the moisture shining on the
> scarlet lips and on the red tongue as it lapped the
> white sharp teeth. Lower and lower went her head.
> I closed my eyes in a languorous ecstasy and waited.
> (ch. 3, p. 44)

Both of these scenes are not-so-subtly charged with a kind of sexual violence that led many to call for the novel to be banned. Harker is approached by three beautiful women and desires to kiss them; Lucy the vampire is "killed" by the man who loves her—a stake driven through her heart and her head lopped off. These scenes are indeed very disturbing. As so often happens, the fictional portrayal of evil in order to show the glory of goodness is problematic—especially for Christians.

Nevertheless *Dracula* mirrors human life in many fascinating ways. In a sense we all take life from life—we eat things that were alive to preserve our own lives.[6] This is part of God's order of things after the Fall—it is a central aspect of the curse of sin. Death is always following closely behind us. Life must be purchased through death.

Vampirism may be seen as a metaphor for how the postlapsarian ("after the Fall") world works, when death is introduced into a world designed for life which is meant to be eternal and joyful. It is a strange revision of Gospel, not quite a reversal but rather a distorting mirror, we might say. Dracula must spill and drink the blood of the innocent in order to achieve his extended life, at the cost of theirs. The eternal Christ, who is life itself, spills his own innocent blood to generously give eternal life to those who are not innocent.

---

6. In Shakespeare's *Hamlet*, the villain and the protagonist discuss the very same thing: "We fat all creatures else to fat us, and we fat ourselves for maggots…" (Act IV, scene iii).

So, what then is the "worldview" of Stoker's novel? Is it Christian, in any sense? Is it pagan? Could it be, somehow, both?

I don't think it could be called "Christian" in the strictest sense, since it does not explicitly advocate a biblical worldview. There are no vampires, werewolves, or undead in God's world. These creatures are imaginative reflections of the things we fear and dread in our nightmares. But in that function they do in fact point to the truth that there are powerful wicked beings who are eternal and hate human life: the demons. Furthermore, vampires derive life from the blood, a trope which goes back into the Old Testament and has its ultimate fulfillment in the spilling of the blood of Christ for his Church. Again, we see a strange, distorted reflection of the truth of the Gospel here.

But in a very real sense we could say the novel's fictionality is true to life in a general way. No, vampires do not literally exist. When you're dead, you're dead. But that is not all there is to it. There is, in fact, good and evil in the world. There is evil that is absolutely, uncompromisingly, adamantly selfish. This evil may well be understood, metaphorically at least, as a malevolent force that preys upon others and destroys their lives. That is how we understand evil in legal matters, moral matters, and spiritual matters. C.S. Lewis's devils in *The Screwtape Letters* are imagined as gluttons feasting on the souls they tempt. Adultery, theft, and lying are all forms of selfish ambition. We punish criminals who damage the lives of others. And those who fight evil, whether externally or internally, are called heroes. Ever since the Fall we have sought to drive stakes through the heart of wickedness, to lop off its head. But we have been unable, as we are fully complicit in evil as fallen humans. We are indeed vampiric in how we treat one another. Therein lies the real terror of *Dracula*—that, after Adam bit into the fruit, all of us have been bitten and are, in a sense, the living Undead.

QUOTABLES

1. "The impression I had was that we were leaving the West and entering the East." ~ Harker (Ch. 1, p. 7)

2. "Denn die Todten reiten Schnell. (For the dead travel fast.)" ~ Harker's companion (Ch. 1, p. 17)

3. "Listen to them—the children of the night. What music they make!" ~ Count Dracula (Ch. 2, p. 21)

4. "Welcome to my house. Come freely. Go safely; and leave something of the happiness you bring." ~ Count Dracula (Ch. 1, p. 18)

5. "Do you not think that there are things which you cannot understand, and yet which are; that some people see things that others cannot? But there are things old and new which must not be contemplate by men´s eyes, because they know—or think they know—some things which other men have told them. Ah, it is the fault of our science that it wants to explain all; and if it explain

not, then it says there is nothing to explain." ~ Professor
Van Helsing (Ch. 14, p. 220)

6.   "The last I saw of Count Dracula was his kissing his
     hand to me; with a red light of triumph in his eyes, and
     with a smile that Judas in hell might be proud of."
     ~ Harker (Ch. 4, p. 63)

7.   "No man knows, till he experiences it, what it is to feel
     his own life-blood drawn away into the veins of the
     woman he loves." ~ Dr. John Seward (Ch. 10, p. 154)

8.   "I have been so long master that I would be master
     still—or at least that none other should be master of
     me." ~ Count Dracula (Ch. 2, p. 29)

9.   "And so you, like the others, would play your brains
     against mine. You would help these men to hunt me
     and frustrate me in my designs! You know now, and
     they know in part already, and will know in full before
     long, what it is to cross my path. They should have kept
     their energies for use closer to home. Whilst they played
     wits against me—against me who commanded nations,
     and intrigued for them, and fought for them, hundreds
     of years before they were born—I was countermining
     them. And you, their best beloved one, are now to me,
     flesh of my flesh; blood of my blood; kin of my kin; my
     bountiful wine-press for a while; and shall be later on
     my companion and my helper. You shall be avenged
     in turn; for not one of them but shall minister to your
     needs. You have aided in thwarting me; now you shall
     come to my call." ~ Count Dracula (Ch. 21, p. 333-334)

21 SIGNIFICANT
QUESTIONS AND ANSWERS

1. What Gothic or horror novels preceded and influenced *Dracula*?

John Polidori published *The Vampire* in 1819;
the story was first composed during the sum-
mer of 1816, alongside Mary Shelley's writing of
Frankenstein at Lord Byron's Villa Diodati on Lake
Geneva. This work is considered the genesis of the
modern vampire narrative. James Malcolm Ryder
published his massive *Varney the Vampire* as a serial
between 1845 and 1847; these kinds of sensation-
alized melodramas were cheaply printed and were
known as "penny dreadfuls." Then in 1871 Sheridan
Le Fanu published his disturbing thriller *Carmilla*,
a short novel about a not-so-subtly lesbian vampire
preying upon a naïve young girl; this work pushed
the edges of literary acceptability right to the limit.

All three clearly influenced Stoker's work and set
the stage for his masterpiece.

2. According to various ancient superstitions and lore,
    what exactly is a vampire?

> The vampire is a human who has been infected by
> vampirism, which comes from being bitten by a
> vampire. One can change slowly or almost instantly
> into a vampire; the change happens when the victim
> dies. The death of the victim/vampire is not perma-
> nent—the corpse is reanimated and at night it goes
> out to search for human blood, which is necessary to
> keep it alive. The vampire is an undead human with
> strong powers, animal instincts, the ability to change
> form, great strength, hypnotic rhetorical abilities, and
> few weaknesses. It cannot bear symbols of the church
> (communion wafers, crosses, and so forth) and is
> repelled by garlic. It can only be killed by having its
> heart penetrated by wood or metal and its head cut
> off and mouth stuffed with garlic. This releases the
> tortured soul back to God. Otherwise the vampire
> lives for centuries in a tortured existence between life
> and death.

3. How does the novel treat differences between East and
    West?

> The West is identified with rationality, science,
> progress, virtue, and certainty. The East is identified
> with superstition, ancient beliefs, magic, and evil.

London and Transylvania are the main locations for this binary view of the world.

4. What other binary oppositions does the novel feature?

Van Helsing is clearly the opposite of Dracula: a hero of science versus a villain right out of ancient superstition. Mina and Lucy are presented as the ideal virtuous women, while the three vampire ladies of Dracula's castle are wicked women characterized by unrestrained bloodlust and sexuality. The cool plainspoken Texan Quincey is a reverse of the mad Englishman Renfield and, ultimately, of Dracula himself.

5. What is meant by the literary term "Gothic"?

The Gothic is closely related to German and English Romanticism, with an emphasis on emotion, irrationality, transcendent experience, terror and horror, and the sublime. These novels became popular in the late eighteenth century and remained so throughout the nineteenth. The rational world of science, objectivity, and sensibility is left behind for a universe of the strange, unexpected, and unknown. Monsters, devils, spirits, the supernatural, and the uncanny all figure into the Gothic, which has remained popular even to the modern day with some of the bestselling authors like Stephen King writing horror fiction that sells tens of millions of copies.

Gothic tends to focus on dread more than gore,
subtlety more than explicitness.

6. How does *Dracula* comment on the society in which it
    is set, late Victorian England?

> The second half of the nineteenth century in
> England was a period of great progress and
> widespread optimism. There were social critics
> and literary works critiquing various social prob-
> lems, but essentially the period was one of positive
> growth across many areas. There was however a
> deep reticence about sexuality, at least in the public
> sphere, alongside a certain fear of the mysterious,
> the invasive, and the barbaric. Stoker's *Dracula*
> brilliantly leverages both of these social realities
> into his unsettling fiction. He subtly foregrounds,
> without being explicit, the strange interrelationships
> between sex, seduction, violence, selfishness, life,
> death, good, and evil.

7. Why can't Dr. Seward correctly diagnose Lucy?

> John Seward is a product of the Western system of
> science and medicine. He looks for objective facts
> that fit into an orderly system describing an orderly
> world. He is not superstitious and does not believe
> in monsters, ghosts, or ghouls. He is thus blind
> to the spiritual reality of personal evil as seen in
> Dracula.

8. Lucy does not die immediately when Dracula attacks her. Why is this?

> Dracula does not always kill his victims outright.
> Some, like Lucy and Mina, are partly drained of
> blood and left alive. Their bodies produce more
> blood food for the vampire—but they slowly begin
> to mutate into vampires themselves.

9. What role does Quincey play in the plot? He seems an anomaly and throwaway character.

> Quincey Morris is a real character but also a
> "type"—just as Van Helsing is the embodiment of
> Rationalism, Holmwood of stoic fidelity, and Mina
> of virtue and wit, the big Texan can be seen as a
> simple-hearted, kind, generous hero, and thus a
> being totally opposite of Dracula. This is the reason
> why Quincey must be the one to put the final stake
> into Dracula.

10. What kind of character is Van Helsing?

> While the Professor is a man of science, he also
> understands that there is more to reality than what
> can be objectively understood by cool rationality.
> He is educated in the best Western tradition, but
> he knows Eastern superstition and lore, and is thus
> the only one who can correctly diagnose a victim
> of vampirism. In this way he proves to be a kind of
> Renaissance man, with universal knowledge and
> skills—he cannot not only diagnose vampirism, he
> can track it down and exterminate it. He under-

stands the limits of rationality—and the limits of
the powers of irrational evil as well.

11. Why does Dracula bring boxes of Transylvanian earth
to London?

Dracula needs to sleep on his "own ground" for
reasons that are never quite explained in detail. He
is what we might call a "chthonic monster "—a
creature of the earth, linked to materiality and
earthiness in a visceral way. While the Bible teaches
that men are made of dust, and return to dust when
we die, vampires are "earth" that does not die—they
take life by draining the blood of the living. In this
way they do not return fully to the earth by decay-
ing. But they still must sleep in the daytime in their
native earth. This is just one of the ways that they
are the "undead."

12. Why does Dracula only drink the blood of females?

This is never clearly explained in the novel. Harker
is attacked by the three vampire women in the
castle, and Dracula feeds on Lucy and Mina (and,
possibly in the past, Renfield). Dracula certainly
had Harker under his power in the castle. Why this
vampiric feeding is apparently "hetero" is an open
question. It could serve as a kind of partial metaphor for selfish sexuality, or it may simply be a plot
device: male vampire feeds on female humans who
are rescued by male humans.

13. The novel changes settings from Transylvania to England, then back to Transylvania for the climax. Why so much motion?

> The story creates a clear bifurcation between locations, characters, and values. The opposition between geographical locations metaphorically reiterates the differences between characters and values. London is the center of rational civilization which is invaded by an Eastern irrational evil in the form of the undead. The evil is beaten back to Transylvania by the heroic efforts of a scientist (Van Helsing) who understands the limits of rationality as well as its strengths. He approaches the Otherness of the Eastern evil undead with the "rationality" of the East—he takes their superstitions about vampires and how to kill seriously.

14. "Ah, it is the fault of our science that it wants to explain all; and if it explain not, then it says there is nothing to explain." What does this mean in the context of the entire novel?

> These lines from Chapter 14 encapsulate the tension between the desire for rational explanations, which are satisfying but never complete, and our sense that there are elements to the universe that are non-rational. Science is faulted for being totalizing, and failing to explain everything that is. This is the classic critique of Modernism.

15. Why does Stoker use an epistolary style for the novel instead of a straightforward narrative?

> Telling the story from numerous viewpoints adds to the suspense and sense of creeping dread; the readers begin to figure out what is going on before many of the characters do. We realize before Harker that he is a prisoner of an evil creature. We know Mina and Lucy, in all their Victorian female innocence, are in danger long before they have any idea what is coming. We know before Dr. Seward what is making Lucy so weak and pale. The ship's log is particularly terrifying in its cold objectivity (Chapter VII).

16. How does foreshadowing work to build suspense?

> From the opening chapters, the reader is constantly presented with a sense of impending danger and doom. We see that Dracula is a foreboding figure not to be trusted, and we fear for Harker. We find out about his plans to move to London even as we learn of Mina and Lucy and their innocent lives in that city.

17. "All men are mad in some way or another, and inasmuch as you deal discreetly with your madmen, so deal with God's madmen too, the rest of the world." Is this an accurate description of mankind?

> In a way humans after the Fall *are* mad. Those who are dangerously crazy are put into institutions by

those who are less crazy, but in the grand scheme
of things all humans have a problem with reality,
with self-awareness, with knowing themselves, with
speaking the truth, and with acting consistently
with what we believe and know to be true. We can
see ourselves in both Dracula and Renfield, in other
words.

18. When does Stoker present Dracula as a sympathetic
    figure—if ever?

This is also an open question. Some film portray-
als of Dracula are at least partially sympathetic,
and many later vampire novels and films make
vampires the heroes, at least in some sense of the
word. While Stoker clearly presents Dracula as
pure, unmitigated evil, unrepentant to the end, it is
possible to have some sense of feeling for him as a
tragic, Romantic figure, doomed to a horrible exis-
tence of preying upon the innocent to procure for
himself a life that is miserable, lonely, and endless.

19. What is the *fin de siècle*, and how does Dracula fit into
    this understanding of cultural history?

The French phrase means "end of the century" and
was popular at the end of the nineteenth century.
Some of Europe's educated cultural elite had grown
pessimistic about progress; others had increased
their optimism. *Dracula* functions along both ap-
proaches: the darkness of the Eastern evil personi-
fied in the vampire is overcome by the rationality of

the West as seen in Van Helsing and his followers. And yet Van Helsing knows he must defeat Dracula using the methods of ancient superstition.

20. *Dracula* is frightening without being merely gory. How does it work differently from modern horror films in this respect?

> Most modern horror films rely on visual shock value to induce fear in their audiences. *Dracula* instead uses dread and suspense which mounts and mounts over a long period of time with no release of tension. When the horrific (and sometimes gory) moments come, the reader is so wound up that it magnifies the effect greatly. Instead of a series of gruesome events we slowly unfold a world of creeping dread.

21. How is *Dracula* similar and different from the other great Romantic/Gothic monster novel, *Frankenstein*?

> Dracula, written by a male author, features an evil male being whose primary action is a kind of seduction and removal of the life force. Frankenstein, penned by a young woman, features a scientific "creator" who makes a human out of dead body parts—he is almost like a "male mother." Both novels are obsessed with the question of life: what is it, where does it come from, how does it end, what does it mean?

FURTHER DISCUSSION
AND REVIEW

Dracula has value because while it is a fantasy horror novel it is realistic and accurate about human nature. It does not paint humans as perfect; even the hero Van Helsing is often vain. But it does show that some humans act better than others do, which is biblically accurate. (This of course does not make them righteous.) On the two extremes we have the virtuous female characters of Mina and Lucy, and the heroic males like Arthur, Quincey, and Dr. Seward, but the titanic opposition is between Professor Van Helsing and Count Dracula (representing at one level the ultimate opposition between good and evil). What makes the story so compelling as that the opposition of good and evil is personal. Again, this is biblically accurate; good and evil are not mere abstract forces, but they are persons in deeply ultimate sense: Christ is goodness itself, and Satan is evil embodied.

For the believer, this kind of narrative is not surprising. As much as we fallen humans suppress the truth, we still know what it is. We know there is good and evil, and we know these categories are personal and not merely abstract. We are revolted by selfish evil and are attracted by heroic sacrifice. This does not mean that we can consistently act according to our ideals, of course—that is the curse of being fallen. We know what is good but we cannot consistently perform it. Instead we do what we know is wrong—even though we hate it, as Paul writes in Romans 7:15–23.

The value of *Dracula* is that it opens up a serious conversation about the reality of evil, the necessity of fighting it, and the terrifying nature of being trapped by our own evil natures as creatures meant for life but doomed to eternal death.

Master what you have read by reviewing and integrating the different elements of this classic.

SETTING AND CHARACTERS

Be able to compare and contrast the personalities (including strengths, weaknesses, and mannerisms) of each character. Which characters change over the course of the novel? Which do not?

PLOT

Be able to describe the beginning, middle, and end of the book along with specific details that move the plot forward and make it compelling.

CONFLICT

Go through the character list and describe the tension between any and all main characters. Then, think about whether any characters have internal conflict (in their own minds). Is there any overt conflict (fighting), or conflict with impersonal forces?

THEME REVIEW

Be able to describe what this classic is telling us about the world. Is the message true? What truth can we take from the plot, characters, conflict, and themes (even if the author didn't believe that truth)? Do any objects take on added meaning because of repetition or their place in the story (i.e., do any objects become symbols)? How does the author use perspective, tone, and irony to tell the truth?

TAKING THE CLASSICS QUIZ

Once you have finished the worldview guide, you can prepare for the end-of-book test. Each test will consist of a short-answer section on the book itself and the author, a short-answer section on plot and the narrative, and a long-answer essay section on worldview, conflict, and themes.

Each quiz, along with other helps, can be downloaded for free at www.canonpress.com/ClassicsQuizzes. If you have any questions about the quiz or its answers or the Worldview Guides in general, you can contact Canon Press at service@canonpress.com or 208.892.8074.

ABOUT THE AUTHOR

Grant Horner is Associate Professor of Renaissance and Reformation Studies at The Master's University. He earned his M.A. at the University of Alabama and has done doctoral work at UNC-Chapel Hill and Duke University. He is the author of the best-selling *Meaning at the Movies*. Grant is also one of just a few climbers to complete the notorious "Nose" route on El Capitan in less than 24 hours (and is the only one to have done so on his first visit to Yosemite Valley). Grant and his wife Joanne have three children and several grandchildren.

www.ingramcontent.com/pod-product-compliance
Lightning Source LLC
Chambersburg PA
CBHW070049040426
42331CB00034B/2863